a gift for

_____

from

_____

WIT & WISDOM

of

MOTHERS

Classic and Contemporary Quotes on Motherhood

GIFT BOOKS
from Hallmark

BOK4133

The Wit and Wisdom of Mothers: Classic and Contemporary Quotes on Motherhood
Manuscript compiled by SnapdragonGroup[SM] Editorial Services
Introductions and additional editorial development by Lauren Benson and Chelsea Fogleman

Published by Hallmark Books, a division of Hallmark Cards, Inc.
Kansas City, MO 64141

Visit us on the Web at www.Hallmark.com.

Printed in China

WIT & WISDOM

of

MOTHERS

Classic and Contemporary Quotes on Motherhood

TABLE *of* CONTENTS

INTRODUCTION

*A*sk anyone to name the most influential people
in his or her life, and chances are, "Mom" will be at or near
the top of the list. Who are these women who have
the power to shape lives so profoundly?

Everybody has a mother, and yet every mother is different,
every parent-child relationship unique. Mom's role is dynamic
and ever evolving as both family life and the world outside
the home change at an increasingly brisk pace.

But whatever a mother's unique personal traits may be, she
is always central in her family's life. And the love, guidance, and
support she shows are valued beyond measure. The quotes
in this book not only celebrate her role as caregiver but also
embrace the patient, dedicated, and fun woman she is. In an
uncertain world, she constantly shines as a source of love
and comfort. No wonder the word "mom" is so significant.
The wonderful moments shared with her last a lifetime.

THERE'S NO LOVE LIKE MOM'S LOVE

*M*eaningful memories of Mom stick with us:

how she always found ways – whether through

a small gesture or a major, well-orchestrated effort –

to show how much she loved her family.

And that kind of love doesn't stop nurturing a child's heart

once grade school is done. A mom's love carries her

children into adulthood, not only shaping the people they

become but also infusing them with the strength to

make tough choices and pursue distant dreams.

Time may change moms, their children, and the relationships

they share, but one thing will remain certain:

Mom is always in your corner.

I got more children than I can rightly take care of,
but I ain't got more than I can love.

Ossie Guffy

When it comes to love, mom's the word.

Anonymous

A mother is the truest friend we have.

Washington Irving

A man loves his sweetheart the most,
his wife the best,
but his mother the longest.

Irish proverb

If only we could see ourselves as mothers do,
we would love ourselves far greater
and with more forgiveness than we could imagine.

Lauren Benson

Behind every successful man, there's a woman he calls mom.

Felicity Martin

Mothers all want their sons to grow up to be President,
but they don't want them to become politicians in the process.

John F. Kennedy

If you can't hold your children in your arms,
please hold them in your hearts.

Mother Clara Hale

There's no way to be a perfect mother
and a million ways to be a good one.

Jill Churchill

Your children need your presence more than your presents.

Jesse Jackson

Only love can be divided endlessly and still not diminish.

Anne Morrow Lindbergh

The greater love is a mother's; then comes the dog's;
then the sweetheart's.

Polish proverb

There is no friendship, no love,
like that of the mother for the child.

Henry Ward Beecher

Oh, what a power is motherhood.

Euripides

Love is, above all, the gift of oneself.

Jean Anouilh

A mother's hug
says to the heart
what a lifetime of words
can never say.

Mary Miró

A mom's heart
is a lot like her purse.
It holds everything
a kid could ever need —
and a little bit extra.

Linda Staten

My mother's love
for me was so
great that I have
worked hard to
justify it.

Marc Chagall

The most important thing in
any relationship is not what you get
but what you give.

Eleanor Roosevelt

A mom's love waits up
when the rest of the world
has already turned out the lights.

Diana Manning

"Mom"
A word that sounds
like a warm hug feels.

Russ Ediger

A rich child often sits in a poor mother's lap.

Danish proverb

A mother is she who can take the place of all others,
but whose place no one else can take.

Cardinal Mermillod

There are two ways of spreading light:
to be the candle or the mirror that reflects it.

Edith Wharton

A mom will sit in the rain
in the bleachers to watch
her kid sit on a bench.

Bill Gray

WHAT A MOM SAYS	WHAT A MOM MEANS
Put on a sweater.	I'm cold.
Young people need their rest.	Go to bed so I can have some peace and quiet.
You're too young to stay out that late.	I'm too old to wait up that late!
Choose your friends wisely.	Ditch the weirdos pronto!
You'll learn a few things when you're out on your own.	The landlord won't let you play your stereo on "STUN" either.
Where are you going?	I LOVE YOU.
Who else will be there?	I LOVE YOU.
When will you be home?	I LOVE YOU.
Be careful!	I LOVE YOU.

Linda Barnes

Mom's hugs are like
peanut butter and
jelly sandwiches...
they're sweet
and they stick with you
a long time.

Kay Andrew

A GOOD MOM LOVES THEM ALL

All jokes cute and colorful,
All stories true and tall,
All prayers sweet and sleepy-eyed...
a good mom hears them all!
All pets lost and lovable,
All playthings great and small,
All clothes tossed and trackable...
a good mom finds them all!
All kids mild and mischievous,
All kids who climb and crawl,
All kids wild and wonderful...
a good mom loves them all!

Ed Cunningham

ALL IN THE FAMILY

Every family circle has little nuances in its habits,

relationships, and values. But one factor always seems

constant: how much "Mom," and later "Grandma," means

to everyone. How many favorite family stories start with

"Like Mom used to say...." or "Remember the time

when Grandma....."? That maternal smile of encouragement,

those words of advice ripple across the generations,

inspiring children and grandchildren alike.

Mom's influence endures. And at the end of the day,

no one can rally the family "troops" like she can.

Her family loves her, enjoys her and — let's face it —

couldn't survive without her.

Other things may change us, but we start and end with family.

Anthony Brandt

What has made this nation great?
Not its heroes but its households.

Sarah Josepha Hale

So sweet and precious is family life.

James McBride

The woman is the heart of the home.

Mother Teresa

No one is poor who has a godly mother.

Abraham Lincoln

Always be nice to your children because they
are the ones who will choose your rest home.

Phyllis Diller

What can you do to promote world peace?
Go home and love your family.

Mother Teresa

Few mistakes can be made by a mother-in-law
who is willing to baby-sit.

Anonymous

Home was the place where magic lived,
and Mom was the one who made it happen.

Anonymous

A mother is a person who, seeing there are only
four pieces of pie for five people, promptly announces
she never did care for pie.

Tenneva Jordan

The family is one of nature's masterpieces.

George Santayana

Moms are the static cling
that makes the little socks
stick to the bath towel
that is family.

Bill Bridgeman

It goes without saying that you should never have
more children than you have car windows.

Erma Bombeck

The best way to keep children home is to make the home atmosphere pleasant — and let the air out of the tires.

Dorothy Parker

I think it must be somewhere written that the virtues of mothers shall be visited on their children.

Charles Dickens

A family is a unit composed not only of children
but of fathers, mothers, an occasional animal
and, at times, the common cold.

Ogden Nash

To a child raised in a loving home,
heaven does not seem like such a faraway place.

M. D. Rhoda

Every family tree must have a little sap.

Anonymous

Govern a family as you would cook small fish – very gently.

Chinese proverb

Be good at "letting go."

Marsha Sinetar

The best part of motherhood is having lots of memories...
and embarrassing the snot out of your kids by
bringing them up as often as possible.

Steve King

I've only got one mom.
Couldn't get by with any fewer,
couldn't handle any more.

John Dill

TOP 10 THINGS HANDED DOWN
FROM MOM TO MOM

10. The loud finger snap that will stop kids dead in their tracks.

9. The "I'm not angry, I'm disappointed" speech.

8. The fine art of the peanut butter and jelly sandwich.

7. The ability to separate mixed modeling clay colors.

6. The rule about not mixing the modeling clay colors.

5. The keen sense that a child is probably sitting
   too close to the TV.

4. The "How do you know you don't like it if you haven't tried it?" line.

3. The appropriate amount of time to spend in the corner.

2. The various comebacks to "But all my friends are doing it."

And the #1 thing handed down from mom to mom...

1. The terrified look that follows the question "Where do babies come from?"

Dee Ann Stewart

Good moms let kids lick the beaters.
Great moms turn the mixer off first.

Amie Doyen

How is it that the mother who could tell
if I was even near a party where someone
smoked a cigarette can't tell when her own
grandchildren are shamelessly kissing up?

Dan Taylor

Having family responsibilities and concerns
just has to make you a more understanding person.

Sandra Day O'Connor

The presidency is temporary – but the family is permanent.

Yvonne de Gaulle

KIDS: A MOM'S PRIDE AND JOY

$\mathcal{K}$ids mean fun times, challenges, mistakes,
and rewards all rolled into one (mostly) endearing little
package. They start out cute and cuddly, needing constant
care and attention, but then, slowly — so slowly that it may
be hard to recognize as it's happening — their unique
personalities emerge.

Then, suddenly, the kids are out shining in the world all by
themselves. Sometimes, Mom thinks that all her worrying
about them will never end (and, of course, it never will),
but she wouldn't trade that right to worry for anything.
Because she knows that although kids will someday step
outside that front door to create their own paths in the
world, they will always remain Mom's pride and joy.

We find a delight in the beauty and happiness of children
that makes the heart too big for the body.

Ralph Waldo Emerson

There is no greater miracle than watching a child being born.

James McBride

Life began with waking up and loving my mother's face.

George Eliot

A mother's arms are made of tenderness,
and children sleep soundly in them.

Victor Hugo

You never get over being a child
as long as you have a mother to go to.

Sarah Orne Jewett

Cherishing children is the mark of a civilized society.

Joan Ganz Cooney

If children grew up according to early indications,
we should have nothing but geniuses.

Johann Wolfgang von Goethe

In most states, you can get a driver's license when you're sixteen years old, which made a lot of sense to me when I was sixteen years old, but now seems insane.

Phyllis Diller

There's nothing wrong with teenagers that reasoning with them won't aggravate.

Anonymous

Before I got married, I had six theories about bringing up children; now I have six children and no theories.

John Wilmot, Earl of Rochester

There are two classes of travel – first class and with children.

Robert Benchley

Mom's the friend you tell 60 percent of everything to.

Dan Taylor

It always struck me as a blessing
that my mom had love at the front of her heart
rather than eyes at the back of her head.

Lauren Benson

"Interruptibility" makes a great mom.

Dee Ann Stewart

Moms give you a middle name so they
can call you by it when they get mad at you.

Anonymous

My mother had a great deal of trouble with me,
but I think she enjoyed it.

Samuel Clemens

A mother's hand
brushes hair from your eyes,
tears from your cheek,
hurt from your heart.

Lauren Benson

Children need love, especially when they do not deserve it.

Harold S. Hulbert

A mom is a woman
whose aim with a thermometer
is unmatched.

Scott Oppenheimer

Mom...the best cheerleader
that vegetables ever had.

Bill Gray

Sometimes motherhood can just make you want to scream!
(So go ahead and scream. They can't hear you anyway.)

Bill Bridgeman

In the eyes of its mother, every beetle is a gazelle.

Moroccan proverb

I do not love him because he is good,
but because he is my little child.

Rabindranath Tagore

"WORKING MOM" AND OTHER REDUNDANCIES

*C*ookies baking in the oven, kids playing quietly in the living room, kitchen counter a sparkling white — mothers in the movies somehow accomplish everything without once losing their tempers or breaking a sweat. In the real world, mothers know the substantial work and effort that go into parenting. Whether or not they go to the office each day, all moms work overtime, all the time, taking care of the people they love most. Searching for a missing shoe before school or telling an extra bedtime story before turning out the lights, moms somehow keep track of everything that needs doing and then do it — no matter what else their schedule may demand. They say that a mother's work is never done, and it never seems to be easy. But every time they hear "Thanks, Mom, you're a lifesaver!" or see that grateful, sheepish smile, they know it's worth it.

The phrase "working mother" is redundant.

Jane Sellman

Squabbling siblings, crayon scribblings,
Lots of in-between-meal nibblings...
That's what moms can handle.
"Ouchie" fixing, cookie mixing,
Standing firm on bad-word nixing...
That's what moms are good at.
Troubleshooting, rubber booting,
Ball game and recital rooting...
That's what keeps moms busy.
Loving, caring, guiding, sharing,
Giving joy beyond comparing...
That's what makes moms special!

Ginnie Job

The optimist sees the glass as half full.
The pessimist sees the glass as half empty.
The mother sees the glass as dirty.

Stan Makowski

A suburban mother's role is to deliver children
obstetrically once, and by car forever.

Peter DeVries

A MOM by any other name
is still THE BOSS!

Carolyn Hoppe

TEN COMMANDMENTS FOR MOTHERS

Thou shalt drive the car pool to the ends of the earth.

Thou shalt find the missing sock.

Thou shalt cut both pieces of cake EXACTLY the same size.

Thou shalt NOT get sick when the kids do.

Thou shalt answer questions about geography, long division, and where babies come from.

Thou shalt walk slowly and carry a big purse.

Thou shalt stop on the highway to rescue the turtle... and give the kids raw hot dogs to feed it.

Thou shalt smile through a zillion recitals and ball games.

Thou shalt not admit thou art related to — much less kiss — thy adolescent in public.

Thou shalt give thyself time to relax and enjoy life.

Ginnie Job

Cleaning your house while your kids are still growing up
is like shoveling the walk before it stops snowing.

Phyllis Diller

Sometimes the strength of motherhood
is greater than natural laws.

Barbara Kingsolver

Childhood is short; regret nothing of the hard work.

Doris Lessing

If you want the rainbow, you gotta put up with the rain.

Dolly Parton

Show me a woman who doesn't feel guilty
and I'll show you a man.

Erica Jong

If evolution really works,
how come mothers have only two hands?

Ed Dussault

Keeping house is like threading beads on a string
with no knot at the end.

Anonymous

It's priceless and rare,
but there's nowhere to buy it,
The thing all moms wish for —
rare peace and quiet!

Jennifer Fujita

There are three little words that always evoke
such strong emotions in all moms:
"more counter space."

Dee Ann Stewart

Being a mom is a lot like being in the circus…
You have to clean up huge messes,
your car is always crammed,
and your big helper in all this is often a clown.

Dan Taylor

If cars were designed by moms...
in case of an accident, clean underwear
would be released with the air bag.

Bill Bridgeman

Housework can't kill you, but why take a chance?

Phyllis Diller

A mom's behind you all the way...
picking up all the junk you left lying around the house.

Anonymous

Service is the rent we pay for the privilege
of living on this earth.

Shirley Chisholm

Being a full-time mother is one of the highest-salaried jobs
in my field, since the payment is pure love.

Mildred B. Vermont

I look back on my life like a good day's work;
it was done and I am satisfied with it.

Grandma Moses

MOTHER KNOWS BEST

Sooner or later, whether or not we admit it,

we realize that Mom really does know best.

She's a woman with an uncanny ability to predict when

we'll be cold outside (she was right about those extra layers)

or tired the next day (shouldn't have stayed out so late).

She even knows when we'll feel icky after a meal

(a "balanced diet" means eating more than just sugar

and more sugar). A mother dispenses her wisdom time

and again in the hopes of keeping us safe and happy.

Eventually, as we learn to follow her advice,

we realize she has done just that.

You couldn't fool your mother on the foolingest day
of your life if you had an electrified fooling machine.

Homer Simpson

My mum should have been a lawyer – she always managed
to persuade me that chores would be fun.

Ethan Hopkins

Lessons learned at a mother's knee last through life.

Laura Ingalls Wilder

My mother told me I was blessed, and I have always
taken her word for it. Being born of —
or reincarnated from — royalty is nothing like being blessed.
Royalty is inherited from another human being;
blessedness comes from God.

Duke Ellington

Dear Mom,

When I was little,
you told me I would get big
and I would have short hair like yours
and I would have short hair like yours
and hum in the grocery store
to Neil Diamond tunes.
I regret to inform you, it has happened.

Jen Kostecki

Nothing gives me more happiness
than seeing pictures of my mother
and seeing myself in her.

Lauren Benson

A mother understands what a child does not say.

Jewish Proverb

My mother is a woman who speaks with her life
as much as with her tongue.

Kesaya E. Noda

Few things are more satisfying than seeing
your children have teenagers of their own.

Doug Larson

I have found that the best way to give advice to your children is to find out what they want and then advise them to do it.

Harry S. Truman

One mother can achieve more than a hundred teachers.

Jewish proverb

An ounce of mother is worth a pound of clergy.

Spanish proverb

My mother drew a distinction between achievement and success. She said that achievement is the knowledge that you have studied and worked hard and done the best that is in you. Success is being praised by others, and that's nice, too, but not as important or satisfying. Always aim for achievement and forget about success.

Helen Hayes

A woman is like a tea bag – only in hot water
do you realize how strong she is.

Nancy Reagan

If you judge people, you have no time to love them.

Mother Teresa

Women, if the soul of the nation is to be saved,
I believe that you must become its soul.

Coretta Scott King

A MOM ALWAYS HAS ALL
THE RIGHT ANSWERS:

"Because I'm your mother, that's why."

"It just is."

"Because it's good for you."

"You're NOT everybody else."

"Because I said so!"

Linda Barnes

The Golden Rule:
Keep Mom happy and you're golden.

Tina Neidlein

100 THINGS I DO (OR DON'T DO)
BECAUSE OF YOU, MOM...

1. Fasten my seat belt.
2. Eat a good breakfast.
3. Sit at least six feet from the TV.
4. Never stick beans in my ears.
5. Use my inside voice.
6. Wear clean underwear.
7. Say "please" and "thank you."

8. Never step on a crack.
9. Separate colors from whites.
10. Chew with my mouth closed.
11. Don't drink from the carton.
12. Look both ways.
13. Never say "@#%!" (Oops! I said it!)
14. Use lots of soap.

15. Don't play ball in the house.
16. Use all four legs on a chair.
17. Never play with electrical outlets. (They're not toys!)
18. Sit up straight.
19. Wipe my feet.
20. Don't run with scissors.
21. Wash fruit.

22. Bundle up.
23. Count to ten when angry.
24. Use sunscreen (high SPF).
25. Know who my real friends are.
26. Use medications only as directed.
27. Never stick a fork in the toaster.
28. Get some fresh air now and then.

29. Never bite off more than I can chew.
30. Don't look a gift horse in the mouth.
31. Change my sheets.
32. Strike a match if necessary.
33. Chew each bite at least ten times.
34. Wear sensible shoes.
35. Clip coupons.

36. Write thank-you notes.
37. Floss.
38. Clip my nails instead of biting 'em.
39. Count my blessings.
40. Keep my nose clean.
41. Don't use the good scissors on aluminum foil.
42. Keep my hands to myself.

43. Don't cry over spilled milk.
44. Say "Pardon?" instead of "Huh?"
45. Observe the five-second rule.
46. Cover my mouth when I cough.
47. Cross at the green, not in between.
48. Treat pets with respect.
49. Use my head for something besides a hat rack.

50. Don't talk with my mouth full.
51. Leave it alone if I don't know where it's been.
52. Don't judge a book by its cover.
53. Hang out with the right kind of people.
54. Read the nutrition information.
55. Look on the bright side.
56. Don't put all my eggs in one basket.

57. Feed a cold.

58. Starve a fever.

59. Or the other way around...I always forget.

60. Leave well enough alone.

61. Keep my elbows off the table.

62. Don't jump on the bed.

63. Mind my Ps and Qs.

64. Save wrapping paper.
65. Put the fork on the left.
66. Pay a few cents more for high quality.
67. Look before I leap.
68. Don't lie down with a lollipop in my mouth.
69. Try to see the good in everybody.
70. Don't fidget.

71. Taste, then salt.
72. Read the fine print.
73. But not in dim light.
74. Try new foods.
75. Don't count my chickens before they're hatched.
76. Keep tissues handy.
77. Say "no" sometimes.

78. Make a grocery list and stick to it.
79. Try, try again.
80. Clean out the fridge now and then.
81. Always have a good supply of breath mints.
82. Act my age, not my shoe size.
83. Put my napkin on my lap.
84. Eat more protein.

85. Eat more fiber.
86. Scrub behind my ears.
87. Tip the bellman.
88. Don't scratch myself in public.
89. Save something for a rainy day.
90. Don't pet strange dogs.
91. Make new friends but keep the old.
92. Check all pockets before doing the wash.
93. If I can't say something nice, don't say anything at all.

94. Keep appointments.
95. Don't pick my nose, my ears, my anything.
96. Let a smile be my umbrella.
97. Don't play with my food.
98. Share.
99. Keep my shoes tied.
100. Love my mom forever and ever!

Scott Emmons

MOTHER'S LITTLE LIST
OF WISDOM

The journey of a thousand miles begins with
"I told you to go before we left!"

If the shoe fits, it will be too small two months later.

For every drop of rain that falls, a flower grows...
and clothes get muddy and raincoats get forgotten
and little feet get wet....

Try a little KINDNESS.
And when THAT doesn't work,
try taking away the computer privileges.

When the going gets tough, the tough hire a cleaning service.

It's all over but the shouting — unless you're hosting a party
for a 5-year-old.

The Hallmark Moms

THINGS YOU KNOW
BECAUSE YOU'RE A MOM...

Almost any food can be made into a casserole.

Some items, like toothbrushes, should NOT be shared.

Most emergency room surgeons double as underwear inspectors.

If you don't know where it's been, don't put it in your mouth.

You'll need the jacket later.

Which clothes are "trampy."

Ice cream always makes it better.

Matt Gowen

THANKS, MOM

A mother's words of reason, encouragement, and love

speak to us all our lives. Armed with words that may prod

or pacify, stimulate or soothe, Mom always seems to know

what we most need to hear. Even when we doubt ourselves,

she shows us the way to succeed and gives us the confidence

to do it. When Mom speaks, we listen. She sees the best in us,

brings out the best in us, and always has our best interests

at heart. For all the little and big ways she guides, protects,

and nurtures, it's time to say, "Thank you, Mom!"

Mama was my greatest teacher, a teacher of compassion, love, and fearlessness. If love is sweet as a flower, then my mother is that sweet flower of love.

Stevie Wonder

My mother said to me, "If you become a soldier, you'll be a general; if you become a monk, you'll end up as the pope." Instead, I became a painter and wound up as Picasso.

Pablo Picasso

Guided by my heritage of a love of beauty and a respect for strength – in search of my mother's garden, I found my own.

Alice Walker

I remember my mother's prayers, and they have always followed me. They have clung to me all my life.

Abraham Lincoln

I shall never forget my mother, for it was she
who planted and nurtured the first seeds of good within me.

Immanuel Kant

All I am I owe to my mother.

George Washington

My mother was the making of me. She was so true
and so sure of me (that) I felt I had someone to live for.

Thomas Edison

The doctors told me I would never walk,
but my mother told me I would – so I believed
my mother.

Wilma Rudolph

Motherhood...the boldest move a woman can make,
the most challenging step she can take,
the dearest gift she can give.

Keely Chace

The heart of a mother is a deep abyss,
at the bottom of which you will always find forgiveness.

Honoré de Balzac

We never know the love of the parent until we become parents ourselves.

Henry Ward Beecher

All the reassurance
that a child could ever need
is written on a mother's face.

Sharon Valleau

Memories of the little things my mother did
that always made me feel loved
are with me, even now.

Cyndi Farson

Children find comfort in flaws, ignorance,
and insecurities similar to their own.
I love my mother for letting me see hers.

Erma Bombeck

The world may judge us by what we've done,
but mothers love us for what we are capable of doing.

Barbara Burrow

Children are likely to live up to what you believe of them.

Lady Bird Johnson

Of all the rights of women, the greatest is to be a mother.

Lin Yutang

She tucked me in at night,
bandaged my owies,
made sure I ate my green beans,
took me on walks,
showed me the world...
And though it was unspoken,
all the while,
she was teaching me
about love.

Chelsea Fogleman

To her daughter, a mother is
a map to life and love,
an emotional support and confidante,
a beautiful example
of giving and understanding,
compassion and kindness.
To her daughter, a mother is
an inspiration.

Lauren Benson

Youth fades, love droops, leaves of friendship fall;
a mother's secret hope outlives them all.

Oliver Wendell Holmes

Mother is one to whom you hurry when you are troubled.

Emily Dickinson

When God thought of mother, He must have laughed with satisfaction and framed it quickly – so rich, so deep, so divine, so full of soul, power, and beauty was the conception.

Henry Ward Beecher

If it weren't for moms,
where would we be?
Probably in the middle of traffic,
talking to some stranger — without
our jackets on!

Myra Zirkle

If you have enjoyed this book,
Hallmark would love to hear from you.

Please send your comments to:
Book Feedback
2501 McGee, Mail Drop 215
Kansas City, MO 64141-6580

Or e-mail us at:
booknotes@hallmark.com